LEGENDS OF WARFARE

AVIATION

TOPGUN

The Navy Fighter Weapons School: Fifty Years of Excellence

BRAD ELWARD

SCHIFFER MILITARY

4880 Lower Valley Road ∎ Atglen, PA 19310

Designed by Justin Watkinson
Technical Layout by Jack Chappell
Type set in Impact/Minion Pro/Univers LT Std

ISBN: 978-0-7643-6014-5
Printed in China
5 4 3 2

Published by Schiffer Publishing, Ltd.
4880 Lower Valley Road
Atglen, PA 19310
Phone: (610) 593-1777; Fax: (610) 593-2002
E-mail: Info@schifferbooks.com
www.schifferbooks.com

For our complete selection of fine books on this and related subjects, please visit our website at www.schifferbooks.com. You may also write for a free catalog.

Schiffer Publishing's titles are available at special discounts for bulk purchases for sales promotions or premiums. Special editions, including personalized covers, corporate imprints, and excerpts, can be created in large quantities for special needs. For more information, contact the publisher.

We are always looking for people to write books on new and related subjects. If you have an idea for a book, please contact us at proposals@schifferbooks.com.

Acknowledgments

The information in this book was taken from interviews with former TOPGUN instructors, graduates, and commanding officers, and from my review of documents obtained from TOPGUN and other archives. There are simply too many people to thank for their contributions, but globally I appreciate everyone's input and assistance, and those individuals will be recognized appropriately in my larger work.

I do specifically thank several individuals who have provided photographs for this publication: Dave Baranek; Boeing Corporation; Ted Carlson / Fotodynamics; John Chesire; Department of Defense; Doug Denneny; Tom Finta; Norman Franks; Hill Goodspeed; Mike Grove; Jamie Hunter; Library of Congress; Rick Llinares; Alexander Mladenov; National Archives; Naval Aviation Museum; Naval Aviation News; Naval Historical Center; Naval Historical and Heritage Command; Peter Mersky; Paul Nickell; Northrop Grumman; Neil Pearson; Jose Ramos; Bill Shemley; Tailhook Association; Tom Twomey; US Navy; Aaron Vernallis; Gary Verver.

For a more detailed discussion of various aspects of TOPGUN, please consult the following works:

Auten, Donald E. *Roger Ball! The Odyssey of John Monroe "Hawk" Smith, Navy Fighter Pilot.* New York: iUniverse, 2006.

Baranek, Dave. *Topgun Days: Dogfighting, Cheating Death, and Hollywood Glory as One of America's Best Fighter Jocks.* New York: Skyhorse, 2012.

"50 Years of TOPGUN," *Proceedings.* Naval Institute Press, September 2019.

Hall, George. *Top Gun: The Navy's Fighter Weapons School.* Novato, CA: Presidio, 1987.

O'Connor, Michael. *MiG Killers of Yankee Station.* Friendship, WI: New Past, 2003.

Pedersen, Dan. *Topgun: An American Story.* New York: Hatchette Books, 2019.

Wilcox, Robert F. *Scream of Eagles: The Dramatic Account of the US Navy's Top Gun Fighter Pilots and How They Took Back the Skies over Vietnam.* Annapolis, MD: Naval Institute Press, 1986.

The author thanks the Tailhook Association and Combat Aircraft magazine, which published the author's TOPGUN articles from which some of these pages were drawn.

Contents

Introduction

The story of TOPGUN—the US Navy Fighter Weapons School (NFWS)—is a complex one, difficult to fit into a small volume. These pages, however, attempt to tell the short version, highlighting some of the most significant developments over the past fifty years. It also provides a strong photographic history, highlighting some of the aircraft that have flown at the school and in Navy adversary squadrons.

Began in the fall of 1968, the NFWS arose out of necessity. Aircrew were dying in the skies of Southeast Asia. The new F-4 Phantom II fighter, with its supersonic speed, revolutionary air-to-air missiles, and powerful radar, had not brought an end to dogfighting. In fact, the Phantom crews were struggling to maintain a 2.5:1 kill ratio against older and less sophisticated MiG-17s and MiG-21s flown by inferiorly trained pilots. Historically, Navy kill ratios stood much higher and even reached 14:1 in the Second World War.

A select group of Navy pilots and radar intercept officers (RIOs) stateside sought a solution for these deficiencies and, with the vision of the Ault Report and the leadership of then Lt. Cdr. Dan Pedersen, developed and implemented a new "Schoolhouse" for teaching advanced air combat tactics. TOPGUN commenced its first class on March 3, 1969, and has since graduated more than 4,400 students. Through adaptation and vision, it has remained relevant for over fifty years despite evolving threats and technology.

Fotodynamics

CHAPTER 1
A Short History of Air Combat

Early fighters featured forward-mounted machine guns and were known as "pusher" planes. The Royal Aircraft Factory F.E.8, shown here, was a single-seat "scout" that appeared in 1916. *UK government*

To best understand TOPGUN's origins, it is necessary to first understand what gave rise to its creation. What history has shown, and what in part led to TOPGUN's formation, is a recurring pattern of learning tactics, forgetting those tactics, and then relearning those same tactics in a new war at great loss of life and treasure. This "cycle of learning and relearning," which manifested itself time and time again during the twentieth century, is something that TOPGUN continues to battle even today, some fifty years after its founding.

The Dawn of Air Combat

When the First World War began in August 1914, military use of aircraft was at best in its infancy. Nations such as Italy and the United States had experimented with aircraft militarily, but these were isolated efforts of a few. Italy had flown reconnaissance missions and even dropped grenades from aircraft during the Italian-Turkish War in the fall of 1911, as had Bulgaria in the First Balkan War of 1912–1913. The United States had used aircraft to monitor Mexican troop movements during the Mexican Revolution. Even so, as late as 1914, few envisioned that aircraft would play such a prominent role in warfare. Indeed, only the French air force had anything resembling a military aviation branch.

In the opening months of World War I, aircraft were used as observation and reconnaissance platforms for locating enemy formations, provided photoreconnaissance and artillery spotting, and assisted with friendly troop movements (called "contact patrol"). These aerial spotters quickly proved their worth—the British benefited greatly from aerial reconnaissance during the First Battle of the Marne (September 1914), while the Germans were aided by aerial reconnaissance during the Battle of Tannenberg on the eastern front (August 1914). Given the successes of aerial observation, something needed to be done to keep enemy aircraft from prying over the front lines.

The answer was obvious—design an aircraft to shoot down enemy reconnaissance aircraft. Although there were many small-arms exchanges between aircraft in the fall of 1914, true fighters did not appear until early 1915. Early designs carrying machine guns appeared in February 1915. Known as "pushers," these aircraft placed the engine and propeller behind the pilot facing backward, allowing an unobstructed forward-firing arc for the machine guns. Soon, specially built aircraft, at first called scouts, were armed with synchronized machine guns and sent into battle to shoot down opposing reconnaissance aircraft and to protect one's own observation aircraft from enemy fighters. From this point forward, the two sides battled back and forth for control of the sky, a concept that would be named air superiority.

The Dr. 1, also known as the Fokker triplane, saw heavy use in the spring of 1918 and was the aircraft flown by Manfred von Richthofen (the "Red Baron") for his last nineteen victories.

Some early US volunteer pilots flew the Nieuport 11, a French design, with the Lafayette Escadrille in 1916–1917.
National Archives

The emergence of fighter aircraft meant that all sides needed to develop tactics for air combat. While Britain had notable tacticians, German pilot Oswald Boelcke, credited with forty air victories, is generally considered the father of air fighting tactics. Boelcke was the first to put his combat experiences into writing—a manual of fighter tactics known as the "Dicta Boelcke" that was distributed to fighter squadrons throughout Germany. Boelcke even recommended a specialized weapons school for teaching fighter tactics, which the German air force eventually created.

The rapid evolution of fighters and tactics was one of the central developments of World War I. While other air missions came into being—close air support, strategic bombing, and interdiction—there was no mistake that achieving air superiority was crucial to all other missions. One writer summarized this point well, stating, "The crucial element in successful or unsuccessful air operations in the First World War had been the gaining of air superiority by fighter aircraft. Without fighter support that would drive off enemy fighters, the interdiction, reconnaissance, and close air-support mission became suicide." To win the battle in the air, one must control it.

Oswald Boelcke is regarded as the father of fighter tactics. He codified his theories into eight principles known as "Dicta Boelcke." *Historical Center*

Britain's fourth-leading World War I ace, Albert Ball, shot down forty-four enemy aircraft before his death at age twenty. *Historical Center*

Interwar Years

Unfortunately, the aerial lessons of World War I were largely lost on most participants during the interwar years. The United States and Britain both pursued strategic-bombing theories, with fighters serving in an ancillary point defense or intercept role. Funds and tactical thought were channeled into developing improved bombers, while little attention was given to the advancement of fighter aviation or related tactics. With new aircraft such as the Boeing B-18, the prevailing thought of the day was that "the bomber will always get through." Some tacticians such as Claire Chennault (famous for leading the American Volunteer Group: the "Flying Tigers") called for more attention to pursuit or fighter aviation, but their voices were drowned out by Army Air Corps leadership. Heavily armed bombers were regarded as able to provide self-defense, thus dispensing with escort fighters all together.

Navy fighter advancements were equally dismal. Naval aircraft were viewed in a support role to the battleships, which were still regarded as the "queens of the fleet." Harkening back to World War I, fighters were viewed as point defense to protect the fleet from enemy reconnaissance aircraft and bombers. However, little thought was given to the tactics for doing so. As with Chennault, a few naval aviators were experimenting with tactics.

To the Navy's credit, however, some of its aviators did much more to prepare Navy fighter forces for the Second World War than did the Air Corps fighter community. As far back as the early 1920s, Navy pilots were trained heavily in deflection shooting—learning to lead a target—which made them quite effective in aerial combat. Pilots trained in deflection shooting were extremely versatile because they could attack from virtually any angle up to full deflection, with a reasonable chance of hitting the target. While deflection shooting was also used by the Imperial Japanese Navy, it did not teach full deflection shots. In contrast, the US Army Air Forces, the Royal Air Force, the German Luftwaffe, and the Soviet Red Air Force all used stern and head-on approaches with minimal deflection angles as the primary attack method.

Additionally, in 1926, after seeing that there were no real tactics for naval aviation, the Navy established "concentration periods" whereby pilots could "test in the air the theoretical answers to practical questions" such as "How far and in what manner should efforts to gain control of the air extend?" Moreover, as war approached, several forward-thinking Navy pilots—namely, John Thach, "Butch" O'Hare, and Jimmie Flatley—were quick studies of the air combat reports coming out of Europe and the Far East and developed tactics to defeat the Japanese Mitsubishi A6M Zero, including the Thach Weave (defensive beam maneuver) and shifting from three- to two-plane combat formations.

The Germans' first purpose-built fighter and the first built with synchronized machine guns, the Fokker *Eindecker* gave the Germans air superiority from mid-1915 through early 1916, a period known as the Fokker Scourge.

The Sopwith triplane had moderate combat success but spawned the Germans to develop the triple-winged Fokker Dr. 1.

World War II

Fighter aviation played a significant role in World War II. Fighter pilots of all countries, with perhaps the exception of Germany, would relearn long-forgotten tactics originally tried and tested during World War I. Moreover, many air leaders quickly relearned that air superiority was the first and foremost goal of all air services and that a capable fighter force, properly trained in the latest tactics, was central to that effort. In Europe, US Army Air Force fighter squadrons recognized the value of separating from bombers they were protecting to engage German fighters away from the bomber streams. Long-range, high-performance fighters capable of reaching Berlin were developed, such as the P-47 Thunderbolt and P-51 Mustang. In the Pacific, F-6F Hellcats began using their energy advantage when tangling with the sharply turning A6M Zero, while Army P-38 Lightnings utilized diving attacks. Hellcat

pilots ended the war with an overall 19:1 kill ratio and a 13:1 ratio against the Zero. In both theaters, pilots began to appreciate the advantages of their aircraft while exploiting the weaknesses of their opponents.

But after World War II, just as happened following World War I, US fighter communities again looked to new technologies and theories for answers and discarded many of the sound teachings that had produced successes in prior wars. With the arrival of the high-speed jet, many again surmised that dogfighting was a thing of the past. Atomic-armed bombers became the most feared weapon. The Navy and the newly minted US Air Force reacted by focusing on long-range interceptors to shoot down Soviet bombers before they could reach the mainland US or a carrier task force. Training for dogfights was largely abandoned. Skilled pilots returned to civilian life, and there was no systemic effort to capture the lessons learned from the war, let alone the individual skills of those who flew in it.

Appearing in 1918, the Fokker D.VII was an outstanding fighter. Unlike its contemporaries, it could dive without fear of structural failure. The D.VII was highly maneuverable, climbed well, and resisted spins. *Library of Congress*

Many in the interwar years felt that heavily defended bombers such as the Boeing B-17 Flying Fortress did not need fighter escort. *National Archives*

Korean War

The 1950–1953 war in Korea saw a limited role for strategic bombing and no role for atomic weapons. Soon, Navy F-9F Panthers and USAF F-86 Sabres were battling Chinese-flown Soviet MiG-15 "Fagots" over northwestern North Korea in what was known as "MiG Alley." US pilots relearned air combat skills lost since World War II and thankfully were aided by large numbers of World War II veterans who quickly applied their former skills to the new jet world and accumulated a 9:1 kill ratio for the USAF against the MiGs. Fighter pilots returned to tactics developed in earlier wars and modified them for higher speeds.

Navy fighters played a rather small role in the overall Korean fighter war. Although the Navy scored the first air-to-air kills of the war on July 3, 1950, and a jet-on-jet kill on November 9, the bulk of the air combat was handled by the USAF's F-86 Sabre force flying out of bases in northern South Korea. Part of this was due to the geographic location of the carrier forces off the southern coast of the peninsula (far away from "MiG Alley"), but the main reason was due to the inferiority of the Navy's main fighter, the F9F Panther, against the MiG-15. USAF F-86s scored a phenomenal 9:1 kill ratio against the nimble MiGs, downing 792 MiGs while losing seventy-eight Sabres. Panthers claimed five MiG-15s while losing two.

Even with these successes, little was done to document what tactics worked or did not work against the MiGs. Most Navy fighter tactics were developed on an individual squadron or air wing level, and a review of action reports from the various carriers and air wings reveals little in the way of sharing of this information. Carrier Air Group Eleven (CAG-11) aboard USS *Philippine Sea* (CV-47) was one of the few air groups to develop a comprehensive pamphlet covering acceptable tactics, and even then, it is not clear that this was widely circulated.

Post-Korean Developments

Despite the large number of MiG engagements during the Korean War, there was no significant postwar effort to develop any standardized means of training pilots in aerial tactics or for passing down information from those who had experience. In most squadrons, tactical information was passed on by trial and error. Bob Rasmussen, a retired Navy captain who flew F-9Fs with VF-51 in the early 1950s and later flew F-8 Crusaders in Vietnam, remembers: "There was really no such thing as formal training in

how to fight an aircraft. The people that were running the squadrons, for the most part, were World War II veterans who had grown up in the naval aviation community during the war years."

Rasmussen's squadron had "a couple of aces in the squadron," referring in part to Navy Hellcat ace Alexander Vraciu, who downed nineteen Japanese aircraft among others. "We were in the fortunate position to learn from them." But Rasmussen said that without the formal training, "I think it was pretty obvious from the experiences of that period, as well as the early period of the Vietnam War, that we had not really formalized the best way to use the fighter aircraft we were flying." Training in the 1950s was "pretty much ad hoc." "You were briefed by your section leader or division leader. 'Take off and do what I do and stay with me.' And the biggest event of the day was usually to go up over an isolated area and mix it up with another squadron without any prebriefing or postbrief, or any real formal education." This method of sharing knowledge "probably lost a lot of the experience that we could have picked up otherwise."

FAGU Improves Training

The Navy established the Fleet Air Gunnery Unit–Pacific Fleet (FAGU-PAC) at Naval Air Station (NAS) El Centro in May 1952, with the stated mission of "'training fleet pilots in all phases of air delivery of ordnance' at an individual and unit level." FAGU operated very similar to how TOPGUN operated from 1969 through 1995—squadrons sent their best tactical pilots to the desert for several weeks of lectures and flying to teach them the latest techniques in air-to-air combat and weapons delivery. Each attending student then returned to his squadron to become a weapons training officer, imparting the knowledge gained during their FAGU experience.

FAGU consisted of three weeks of lectures and flying. Lectures included briefings on offensive and defensive tactics; weapons delivery methods for bombs, rockets, and strafing; and deflection shooting. Flying reinforced the subject matter discussed during lectures. The instructors made heavy use of postflight debriefings to instill the lessons taught during the lectures and to point out where students could do better during their flights. Graduates of each class were given a FAGU patch—a small, round patch with a black-and-white bull's-eye—a certificate, and some handouts to take back to their squadrons for teaching. Training programs were oriented by aircraft type (similar to the Air Force Weapons School today), with flight training syllabi for each.

Instructors were selected on the basis of recommendations from their former squadron skippers, which was based on their piloting and teaching abilities. "Most of our emphasis when I was there was on tactics rather than weaponry." Many of the FAGU instructors had been to the USAF Fighter Weapons School, and the bulk of the tactics taught came straight from Frederick "Boots" Blesse's *No Guts, No Glory* manual used by the Air Force.

FAGU was disestablished in 1960.

1950s Generally

Advances in missile technology during the 1950s promised an end to dogfights. Fighters could launch, speed to their stations, fire their long-range missiles at approaching bombers, and return to base. The Navy embraced this approach, designing its next fighter/interceptor without a gun. Armed with four Sparrow radar-guided medium-range missiles and four Sidewinder heat-seeking short-range missiles, the F-4 Phantom was made to shoot down long-range Soviet bombers before they could reach US carriers. The Air Force also adopted the F-4 for a similar role.

F-4 aircrews—a pilot and a radar intercept officer (RIO)—were trained in intercept tactics, often trail formations, where the first Phantom detected the approaching bomber while the trailing Phantom obtained radar lock and engaged with a Sparrow. Air-to-air combat tactics—dogfighting—was deemphasized and, in some circles, was even forbidden. Training syllabi of the early 1960s included only a handful of true dogfighting techniques. But even then, crews were not taught to fly their machines to the fullest extent nor were they taught to take advantage of their opponent's weaknesses.

At this point, what vestiges of dogfighting skills that remained rested with the reserve squadrons and the Navy's F-8 Crusader community, the latter of whom aptly dubbed themselves the "Last of the Gunfighters." The F-8, a highly maneuverable supersonic day fighter developed after the Navy's dismal performance against the MiG-15 during the Korean War, carried guns as well as two to four Sidewinder missiles. F-8 pilots cherished their role and spent much of their time dogfighting one another for squadron bragging rights.

It was at this juncture that USAF aircrew and naval aviators entered the Vietnam War. Once again, dogfighting, or by then called air combat maneuvering (ACM), was considered a thing of the past. This mindset would soon prove troublesome for US aircrew over the skies of North Vietnam, since the USAF and Navy were once again poised to relearn the lessons of its former wars. In this war, however, relearning these lessons would come at a considerable cost, in manpower, assets, and national pride.

The Messerschmitt Bf 109 fighter proved its worth during the Spanish Civil War and served the Germans well in the opening days of World War II. *National Archives*

The Japanese Zero (Mitsubishi A6M) was a nimble fighter capable of tights turns but was not heavily armed. It ruled the skies of the Pacific until the F4F Hellcat arrived. *National Archives*

Special "weave" tactics were developed that made a section a F4F Wildcats a match for the Japanese Zero. *US Navy Historical Center*

The "Thach Weave," developed by John Thach, is a tactical-formation maneuver where two aircraft weave in intersecting flight paths to lure an enemy into focusing on one plane. The targeted pilot's wingman would then "weave" into position to attack the pursuer. *National Archives*

David McCampbell was the Navy's top ace during the Pacific War, shooting down thirty-four Japanese aircraft, including nine in a single mission on October 24, 1944. *US Navy Historical Center*

The Hellcat appeared in mid-1943 and helped the Allies obtain air superiority over the Japanese in the Pacific. Over half of all Navy / Marine Corps kills were scored by the F6F. *US Navy Historical Center*

The North American P-51 Mustang dominated the skies over Europe, especially once the aircraft were fitted with long-range drop tanks to allow them to escort bombers deep into Germany. *National Archives*

The P-38 served in Europe, the Mediterranean, and the Pacific and became a strong fighter once crews learned to take advantage of its speed and used it as a slashing fighter. *National Archives*

The German Focke-Wulf Fw 190 was a formidable fighter. The top photo shows a captured Fw 190 as tested by the US Navy in March 1944. This was an early effort to conduct Dissimilar Air Combat Training (DACT). The bottom photo is an Fw 190 that mistakenly landed in England. *Naval History and Heritage Command*

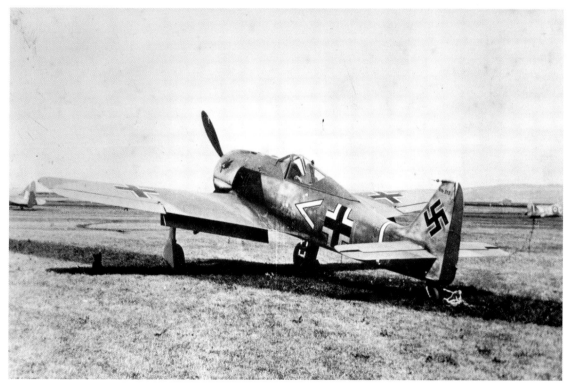

Chinese-flown Soviet MiG-15 Fagots helped remind US fighter pilots that dogfighting skills were not passé even with the advent of high-speed jets. *National Archives*

A captured MiG-15 was painted in American markings, then evaluated against Sabres and Panthers. *NAM*

William "Bill" Amen of VF-111 "Sundowners" scored the Navy's first MiG kill in a Panther, in November 1950. *Grumman*

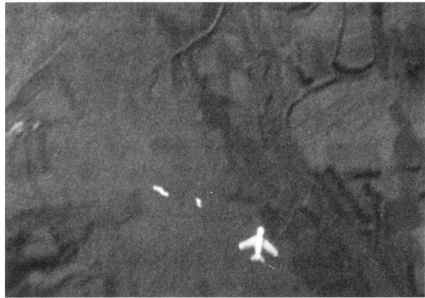

Gun camera footage of Amen's MiG kill. *Grumman*

USAF North American F-86 Sabres scored a kill ratio of better than 9:1 versus Chinese- and Soviet-flown MiG-15s during the Korean War and reinvigorated the concept of dogfighting. *National Archives*

This image shows an F-86 in testing in 1947. *NAM*

The McDonnell F3H Demon was a carrier-based day fighter of the 1950s that carried a gun and missiles. *US Navy Historical Center*

The Navy's answer to the MiG-15, the Vought F-8 Crusader, was an excellent supersonic fighter capable of tight maneuvering. Armed with four 20 mm cannons, it could carry up to four Sidewinder missiles. This Crusader is from VF-32 "Swordsmen" in 1958. *Mersky*

An F3H Demon armed with four AIM-7 medium-range radar-guided Sparrows ca. 1958. Missiles were heralded as signaling the end of the classic dogfight, but experiences in Vietnam would soon prove otherwise. *NAM*

Four AIM-9 Sidewinder heat-seeking missiles can be seen on this Grumman F9F-8 Cougar. *Grumman*

The Fleet Air Gunnery Unit (FAGU) was a precursor to the Navy Fighter Weapons Schools and trained crews in gunnery and air-to-air tactics. Graduates of the three-week course received this patch. *Author*

CHAPTER 2

The Founding of a Legacy

One of the most striking differences between the air services in the post-Korean War / pre-Vietnam War era involved documentation of air combat theory and standardized training. The Navy, as mentioned, operated FAGU but did little otherwise to document appropriate air combat tactics and even less to teach them. The USAF, on the other hand, did a marginally better job. The USAF created the Fighter Weapons School (FWS) in 1954 at Nellis Air Force Base (AFB), Nevada, which focused on developing fighter tactics. Despite promising developments in its early years, the FWS's teachings were soon ignored in favor of Strategic Air Command–dominated bomber theory, which took over Tactical Air Command.

Two Air Force scholars on tactics also emerged. Frederick "Boots" Blesse's initial work, *No Guts, No Glory*, was widely disseminated through both services during the mid- to late 1950s and marked the first publication in either service to attempt to standardize tactics and tactical training. Up to that time, there was virtually nothing published about aerial combat. Blesse's manual, based on his experiences in Korea, stressed the concept of mutual support, provided specific advice for offensive and defensive operations, and set out ground rules for combat in a manner never before attempted. Many Navy squadrons used Blesse's writings as the basis for their air-to-air training. John Boyd's writings on tactics emerged in two phases, the first in a 1956 article in the *Fighter Weapons Newsletter* titled "A Proposed Plan for Ftr. vs. Ftr. Training," which was not a training manual per se, but rather insights into a new way of thinking on air combat training, and the second, dubbed the "Aerial Attack Study," in 1959–1960, which led to a rewrite of the USAF tactical manual. No comparable tactic pronouncements existed in the Navy during the 1945–1960 time frame. Indeed, the first widely distributed Navy tactics advanced manual appears to be that written by future MiG killer Lou Page of VF-21 "Freelancers" in mid-1966.

Implications of FAGU's Closure on the Vietnam War

The disestablishment of FAGU was a watershed moment for the Navy with respect to air combat training and tactical development. When FAGU closed its doors, the Navy was on the verge of transitioning its carrier-based fighter force from a mix of F8U day fighters and F3H all-weather interceptors to the new F-4 Phantom II. FAGU's loss was felt across the fleet, but many of its concepts were soon to resurface in the form of the Navy Fighter Weapons School, otherwise known as TOPGUN.

Vietnam Air War

The air war component of the Vietnam War commenced with Operation Rolling Thunder in early 1965. The first official Navy MiG kill came on June 17, 1965, when an aircrew from VF-21 "Freelancers" downed a MiG-17 by using an AIM-7 Sparrow, in a textbook shoot-down. But this soon proved nonindicative of the true situation. Navy F-4 crews soon found themselves struggling to maintain air superiority versus older MiG-17s flown by poorly trained North Vietnamese pilots. Missiles failed or were launched out of effective firing envelopes, and crews continually played into the MiGs' turning advantage. Despite the superiority of US Navy fighters and weapons, at least on paper, the F-4 kill ratios paled in comparison to prior wars. The F-8 community fared much better, as evidenced in the exchange rates from 1965 to 1968, when Crusaders scored nineteen kills for three losses, achieving a kill ratio of roughly 6.3:1. For the same period, Navy F-4 Phantoms posted a mere 3.2:1 ratio, and those of the USAF F-4s were even lower.

The Navy Reacts

In 1968, following three years of dismal air-to-air kill ratios against the North Vietnamese fighters, the Navy commissioned a study led by Capt. Frank Ault to investigate the underlying cause of the poor Navy fighter and missile performance. Ault's 480-page report, officially titled the *Report of the Air-to-Air Missile System Capability Review*, made 242 recommendations, but the most significant called for the formation of a graduate-level program to teach advanced fighter tactics, something that Captain Ault had concluded was lacking in current fleet squadron and training command syllabi. Ault also called for the development of instrumented training ranges.

Ault's observations, to some degree, were already known by West Coast fighter crews, many of whom were fresh from combat deployments in Southeast Asia and who now populated VF-121 "Pacemakers," the West Coast F-4 Replacement Air Group (RAG) located at NAS Miramar in San Diego, California. These crews were well aware of the Navy's shortsightedness in designing a fighter without a gun, and their overreliance on newly developed but unproven missile technologies.

TOPGUN Formed

On the basis of Ault's report and the outcry of the fighter community at Miramar, the Navy authorized the stand-up of a graduate-level fighter weapons school as a department within VF-121, under the leadership of Lt. Cdr. Dan Pedersen. Beginning in late September 1968, Pedersen, an accomplished pilot who led VF-121's prized Tactics Phase Section, selected four pilots (Mel Holmes, Jim Ruliffson, John Nash, and Jerry Sawatzky) and four RIOs (J. C. Smith, Jim Laing, Darrell Gary, and Steve Smith) and added intelligence officer Chuck Hildebrandt, then set about developing the new tactics and training syllabus. All except Hildebrandt were instructors with the "Pacemakers," and all had combat experience. RIOs J. C. Smith and Jim Laing were MiG killers. These nine men rewrote fighter tactics and developed an instructional method for passing that information on to students that survives even today.

TOPGUN Model

The TOPGUN model called for each squadron to send its best crew—one that was tactically proficient and could teach others—to the then-four-week course where students engaged in academics and flights designed to reinforce the academics. Instructors provided the lectures and flew adversary "red air" against the students, using air assets (namely TA-4F Skyhawks) borrowed from co-Miramar-located VA-126 "Bandits." Upon graduation, the freshly patched graduates returned to their squadron to impart their knowledge of the latest tactics to their squadron mates, and in many cases serving as training officers.

TOPGUN's first classroom was in an abandoned two-room construction trailer "obtained" by crafty bartering. Funds were short; the instructors had no aircraft or furniture, and the instructors even had to type their own manual. Most people viewed the effort as destined to fail. But the instructors pushed on, digging deep into their subject areas and devising new tactics and the means to disseminate those to the fleet. Concepts such as "loose deuce" formations and reliance on the short-range Sidewinder were stressed, as was intimate knowledge of one's own aircraft and the weaknesses of the enemy. The initial class commenced on March 3, 1969, and by 1970, each Pacific Fleet fighter squadron and most Atlantic Fleet squadrons had a TOPGUN-trained aircrew. TOPGUN not only sought to teach advanced tactics to those who would train the fleet, but made it a point to retain the lost lessons of the past.

TOPGUN's First Kill and 1972 Operations

A TOPGUN-graduate-led crew scored a kill on March 28, 1970, downing a MiG-21. Jerry Beaulier, a graduate of Class 01-69, piloted the VF-142 "Ghost Riders" Phantom. At this point, the fleet was excited about TOPGUN's teachings, but there were still doubters, including some at the school who questioned whether their message was truly getting out. The performance of Navy fighter crews during the 1972 Operation Linebacker campaign, however, provided all the validation TOPGUN needed. Navy aircrews, largely TOPGUN graduates, downed twenty-six North Vietnamese MiGs with only two losses, achieving a kill ratio of 12.5:1. Three MiGs were downed on a single day by the Navy's only ace crew of the war, Randy "Duke" Cunningham and Willie "Spartan" Driscoll. At the same time, USAF fighters maintained virtually the same ratio (1.78:1) it had experienced during Rolling Thunder from 1965 to 1968. TOPGUN had proved a major success.

TOPGUN was made a detachment in January 1971, and on July 1, 1972, the school became an independent command under the leadership of Cdr. Roger Box.

The Navy began the 1960s with the F-4 Phantom as the fleet's long-range interceptor. Here, Phantoms from VF-84 "Jolly Rogers" fly near NAS Oceana. *US Navy Historical Center*

Only a handful of MiG-19s "Farmers" were encountered by Navy fighters. Two MiG-19s would fall to Navy fighter crews in 1972. *National Archives*

The MiG-21 Fishbed represented the top-of-the-line Soviet fighter and was a true interceptor. It was known for making high-speed slashing attacks on formations, before speeding off. Navy F-4 crews downed six Fishbeds during Rolling Thunder (1965–1968). *National Archives*

Known as "Fightertown USA," NAS Miramar in San Diego was home to the Navy's West Coast F-4 Phantom and F-8 Crusader squadrons. Almost all fighter squadrons sent to Vietnam came from the West Coast. It soon became a mecca of tactical thought, as returning aircrew from Vietnam began sharing their combat experiences. TOPGUN was a perfect addition to Miramar's fighter culture. *Denneny*

Crusader pilots downed nineteen MiGs during the Vietnam War, for a 6:1 kill ratio. The "Last of the Gunfighters" confirmed that ACM training was still relevant in the missile age. This USMC VMFA(AW)-235 Crusader carries rockets and bombs. *NAM*

The difficult-to-see A-4 Skyhawk proved to be an excellent adversary aircraft and presented a similar flying profile as the MiG-17. This made the A-4 the aircraft of choice for training aircrew heading to Southeast Asia. *Mersky*

TOPGUN borrowed two-seat TA-4s from VF-126 "Bandits," then an instrument-training squadron co-located at NAS Miramar. *Fotodynamics*

The AIM-9B Sidewinder locked onto the heat signature of enemy aircraft but had to be fired at the aircraft's exhaust or from behind the target. It proved difficult to obtain and maintain missile lock when the host aircraft was maneuvering hard and under heavy Gs. Later models, such as the AIM-9L and beyond, were all-aspect missiles, meaning they could be fired from any angle. The current version is the AIM-9X Block II. *US Navy*

TOPGUN was given little funds, no equipment, and no aircraft. Steve Smith, one of the founding instructors, "obtained" an abandoned two-room construction trailer on base, which served as the TOPGUN office and classroom until 1970. *Tailhook*

The nimble A-4 proved an excellent stand-in for the MiG-17 and provided aircrew with a DACT adversary representative of the air situation in Southeast Asia. Here, an A-4 maneuvers against an F-4 Phantom. *Verver*

This image features the cover of the TOPGUN manual circa June 1969, roughly the time of the third class. Samual L. Vernallis was an instructor in mid-1969. *Aaron Vernallis*

TOPGUN graduated its first class (01-69) in early April 1969; a total of six classes graduated during that year. *Tailhook*

VAdm. William "Bush" Bringle sits with VF-121 and TOPGUN instructors in the infamous TOPGUN trailer ca. 1970. *Tailhook*

Since TOPGUN was a department within VF-121, its instructors shared duties between TOPGUN and VF-121. All instructors were from the "Pacemakers"' tactics division. *NAM*

VF-121 ADVANCED TACTICS FLIGHT INSTRUCTORS 1969
Original "TOPGUN" Instructors listed in bold with "Call Signs"

Back Row L-R: Jerry Kinch, Dick Moody, Peter Jago, Tom Irlbeck, **Darrell "Condor" Gary** Ross Anderson, **Jerry "Ski" Sawatzky**, Sam Vernallis, Don Sharer, **Jim "Hawkeye" Laing**

Front Row L-R: Joel Grafffman, **Steve "Rebel" Smith, Mel "Rattler" Holmes**, Hank Halleland **Dan "Yank" Pedersen**, Vern Jumper, **Jim "Cobra" Ruliffson, John "Smash" Nash J.C. "Mississippi Two-Five Thousand" Smith** (not in photo)

The now-famous TOPGUN patch was designed at the Miramar Officers' Club by instructors Mel Holmes and Steve Smith on a napkin. It is now world renowned as a symbol of excellence. *Author*

CHAPTER 3
The Rest of the Story

The 1970s: TOPGUN Expands

The early part of the 1970s can best be described as a period of validation and survival. As discussed earlier, TOPGUN's first two years saw much success in producing graduates, which seemed to be making an impact in the fleet. But aside from the March 1970 engagement, the lack of any meaningful air combat opportunities in Southeast Asia prevented a wholesale validation of TOPGUN's teachings. Of course, that validation came in 1972 through a 12.5:1 kill ratio against North Vietnamese MiGs, and went a long way toward silencing the school's naysayers.

Even with the school's new command status in hand, however, the early 1970s presented many challenges. Physical space, one of the school's early foes, was addressed in 1970, when it moved from its original two-room trailer to Hangar 2 at Miramar. But forces still tried to close or at least reduce the stature of the school, arguing that the war was now over and, with postwar budget cuts, there was no need for TOPGUN. In late 1973, the school faced an existential threat when it lost all but one of its adversary aircraft (by this time it had acquired a small stable of A-4E Skyhawks of its own) to the Israelis, who requested them to replace losses in the Yom Kippur War. Last-minute politicking by then skipper Ron "Mugs" McKeown saved the day by obtaining a small number of Northrop T-38 Talons abandoned by the Air Force, as well as two A-4s from the Marine Corps.

In 1972–73, TOPGUN gained access to instrumented ranges, something the Ault Report had recommended, which allowed sophisticated training on missile employment and took all guessing out of air-to-air training. No longer could crews argue who "won" a mock engagement—the Air Combat Maneuvering Instrumentation/Range (ACMI/R) answered that question and validated all missile shots. ACMI/R ranges were located at Marine Corps Air Station (MCAS) Yuma, Arizona, and monitors were at Miramar.

By 1975, the TOPGUN fighter course had expanded to five weeks, and the school boasted up to seventeen staff instructors. Although originally including one week of air-to-ground instruction, this had been dropped in 1970, and all five weeks were pure air-to-air instruction. While continuing to teach its mainstay fighter course, TOPGUN added an air-intercept controller (AIC) curriculum in 1972–1973, classes for NATO country air forces in 1974, and adversary pilot instruction in 1975. The AIC program sought to integrate air controllers, who had experienced successes during the Vietnam air war in controlling MiG intercepts, to familiarize AICs with fighter tactics. The adversary program was driven by then commanding officer Jim Ruliffson, who sought to standardize the newly expanding fleet adversary squadrons. To be effective and safe, adversary pilots had to be trained in similar threat presentations and taught to teach, rather than simply defeat, their fleet adversaries.

TOPGUN was firmly established and growing by the mid- to late 1970s. The school received brand-new adversary aircraft, the Northrop F-5E/F Tiger II, in 1975, which allowed the instructors to simulate supersonic threats such as the MiG-21. The school welcomed the new F-14 fleet interceptor, with the first Tomcat students arriving in Class 07-76. That same year it also added a maritime air superiority course, TOPSCOPE, aimed at teaching F-14 Tomcat RIOs advanced fleet defense training against long-range, antiship-missile-armed Soviet bombers threatening US carriers. This course took advantage of the Tomcat's long-range AWG-9 radar and AIM-54 Phoenix missile and ran for four years.

To accommodate the growing staff, as well as provide classrooms for its new TOPSCOPE program, TOPGUN moved into Hangar 1 in late 1977. Finally, to expose students to the actual threats faced overseas, TOPGUN sent its students to fly against the secret MiGs at Tonopah (4477th). This provided much-needed first exposure to MiG-17, MiG-21, and MiG-23 fighters, building confidence and reducing the impact of encountering an enemy aircraft.

The Navy had only one ace crew during the Vietnam War. Pilot Randy Cunningham and RIO Willie Driscoll downed five MiGs between January and May 1972, including three in one day on May 10. Both went on to become instructors at the school. *US Navy Historical Center*

The A-4 served as TOPGUN's sole adversary aircraft until late 1973, when the school acquired a small fleet of ex-USAF T-38s. During the graduation strike, the Skyhawks were occasionally supplemented by other dissimilar aircraft, such as Navy and Marine F-8s, USAF Reserve F-86s, and USAF Air Defense Command F-106s. *Mersky*

Once TOPGUN was up and running, its instructors were selected largely from former graduates. Outstanding students were placed on a "wish" and then "want" list, observed upon their return to the fleet, and then invited back to serve a two-to-five-year instructor term. Instructors were selected on the basis of their piloting/RIO and tactical skills, but also on their ability to teach others. TOPGUN valued the ability to deconstruct a training mission and extract critical lessons learned as teaching points. Honing these skills, as well as developing a subject matter expertise through long hours of study and TOPGUN's notorious "Murder Board" process, where lectures are fully vetted by the staff, created a culture of excellence on the staff that has survived through today.

The 1980s: TOPGUN's Heyday

The school expanded in size, stature, and impact during the 1980s and became the ultimate source for fleet fighter tactics. To start, in 1980, the TOPSCOPE course was merged into the primary fighter course, referred to as the Power Projection course, under the topic of maritime air superiority and related lectures. But due to the growing complexity of technology and the need to get information to the fleet faster, many of these topics were packaged into a traveling one-week course, Fleet Air Superiority Training (FAST), and presented at NAS Miramar and Oceana. Beginning in 1981, FAST trained F-14 and E-2 Hawkeye squadrons in fleet defense and the outer air battle and involved roughly twelve lectures and simulator periods and an eight-hour battle-group defense simulation. FAST ran through 1994.

The early 1980s saw the arrival of students flying the newly introduced McDonnell Douglas F/A-18 Hornet strike-fighter, while the late 1980s saw the last class featuring the venerable F-4 Phantom. The Hornet quickly proved a formidable fighter, and soon mixed tactics were being developed for F-14 and F/A-18 sections. Night tactics were introduced in the middle of the decade, as well as more advanced surface-to-air tactics, specifically AGM-88 HARM antiradiation missile employment. New tactics were also devised to defend against the emerging forward-quarter threat from MiG-23 Flogger and its all-aspect AA-7 Apex missile, as well as the then-new MiG-29 Fulcrum and Su-27 "Flanker" fighters.

In October 1985, TOPGUN became an Echelon II Command reporting directly to the chief of naval operations. This change, which ushered in command of the school by a Navy captain, brought even more prestige as the school became heavily involved in industry (advising on aircraft and weapons requirements), aircraft evaluation, fleet adversary training, senior officer refresher training, and air wing work at STRIKE U. Two years later, TOPGUN received its first fourth-generation adversary aircraft, the F-16N, which allowed instructors to simulate newer threats such as the MiG-29 and Su-27. All F-5E/Fs were retired shortly after the F-16Ns arrived.

The 1980s also brought worldwide attention to the school from the Paramount movie *Top Gun*. Although the school had been long well known within the military aviation circles, the movie put the real TOPGUN on the map as far as the general public's awareness was concerned, and gave rise to many future naval aviator careers. The Navy also scored the first enemy kills since the end of the Vietnam War, downing two Libyan fighters both in 1981 (Su-22s) and 1989 (MiG-23s). In all, TOPGUN was at the peak of its power, touching all aspects of naval aviation and industry.

The 1990s: Times of Change

Three major events occurred in the 1990s that shaped not only TOPGUN but all naval aviation and are still felt even today. First, in 1994 TOPGUN reintroduced air-to-ground instruction. When the decade began, TOPGUN's course was five weeks long and still exclusively air-to-air combat training. However, the 1991 Gulf War, where aircraft faced little air-to-air threat, demonstrated that air-to-ground or "strike" was the mission of the future. With the Navy moving to more strike fighters (the F/A-18 and the bombing version of the F-14), TOPGUN began incorporating air-to-ground lessons into the syllabus. This expanded the course from five to six weeks.

Second, in 1995 (Class 03-95), TOPGUN implemented the Strike Fighter Weapons and Tactics (SFWT) program and restructured its Power Projection course into a Strike Fighter Tactics Instructor (SFTI) course to train a dedicated squadron-training officer. However, unlike the Power Projection course model, where aircrew immediately returned to their squadrons after completion of the course, SFTIs, upon graduation, are sent to one of several possible destinations where they serve as instructors: the coastal weapons schools, a fleet replenishment squadron (FRS), TOPGUN staff, STRIKE U., or a test-and-evaluation (VX) squadron. Each SFTI finished the remainder of the three-year shore assignment as an instructor and then returned to the fleet as an experienced squadron-training officer.

TOPGUN became an independent command in July 1972, and at that time took possession of a small number of A-4E Skyhawks. Here, BuNo 150090, seen in July 1972, is painted in three-tone blue camouflage. *Grove*

In mid-1970, TOPGUN moved out of its trailer and into Hangar 2, where it remained until the fall of 1977. *Fotodynamics*

VF-126 "Bandits" was redesignated an adversary squadron and provided adversary for fleet units for years to come. TOPGUN worked with the squadron to develop their adversary skills and from time-to-time borrowed their A-4s for instructor use. *Fotodynamics*

SFWT established standards for becoming a combat wing, section lead, and division lead, as well as instructor. The program arose because of inconsistencies in squadron tactical proficiency, often within the same air wing. And while some of this variance was due to differences in individual training officers, some resulted from squadron commanding officers who resisted TOPGUN's teachings and placed their TOPGUN graduates in administrative duties far from tactical instruction. As a result, graduates were unable to spread the concepts taught at the school.

The SFWT program is now utilized by all naval aviation communities and, as of 2016, has been adopted for the Navy's surface fleet. Each aviation community, from maritime patrol to helicopter to airborne early warning, has its own weapons and tactics instructor (WTI) program, and all but the maritime community has a teaching schoolhouse at NAS Fallon as a part of the Naval Aviation Warfighting Development Center (NAWDC; formerly Naval Strike and Air Warfare Center [NSAWC]).

The third major event came in May 1996, when TOPGUN relocated to NAS Fallon and became part of the NSAWC. TOPGUN, once an Echelon II Command, was now one of several departments along with STRIKE U. (NSAWC), and the Carrier Airborne Early Warning Weapons School (TOPDOME), which reported to the two-star admiral commanding NSAWC. Although TOPGUN lost some of its autonomy as a result of the move, most instructors acknowledge that flying at the NAS Fallon instrumented ranges is even better than at Miramar and Yuma, and the opportunity to work closely with the other types of weapons schools and STRIKE U. is invaluable. Interestingly, TOPGUN had considered relocating to Fallon in the late 1970s and again in the early 1980s but then declined.

For the remainder of the 1990s, TOPGUN continued to develop and improve its SFTI program and implement its larger SFWT program, providing standardized training for all fleet squadrons. At one point, roughly from 1998 through 2003, TOPGUN ran a separate five-week Power Projection course for Marine students and a ten-week all-Navy SFTI course. Fleet resistance to the SFWT concept, which initially was rather fierce because it threatened squadron leadership autonomy, soon gave way as the results spoke for themselves. One point of interest is that TOPGUN's F-16N adversary aircraft, which developed cracks due to their heavier-than-anticipated use, were retired in 1995.

Once in their new hangar, TOPGUN painted the walls of the stairway to commemorate each of the Vietnam-era F-4 MiG kills. Each silhouette denotes the MiG type, date of the kill, and name of the aircrew. *US Navy*

2000–2009: New Technologies / New Threats

Overseas operations had a major impact on the school during this decade. Air operations in Afghanistan and Iraq were largely air-to-ground, which led to an even-greater emphasis on instruction on air-to-ground weapons, tactics, and delivery. TOPGUN incorporated more urban close-air support (UCAS) and improved strafing recommendations and tactics, distributing this information through its course and to the fleet. Air-to-air tactics underwent a major revision during the middle part of the decade, driven by evolving foreign threats and the USAF's lackluster performance in its 2004 Cope India exercise. Much of 2004–2006 was spent refining and disseminating these new air-to-air tactics to the fleet.

The year 2001 saw the arrival of the F/A-18E/F Super Hornet, which brought with it changes to the course curriculum and a need to develop new tactics that was better suited for the E/F. TOPGUN unfortunately was a little behind the game in this respect, since it was not given early access to the aircraft and did not have sufficient time to fully vet the aircraft and develop new tactics. The true advancement in Super Hornet tactics did not come until the middle part of the decade, when the new Block IIs were released to the fleet. This time, with the help of several West Coast Block II Super Hornet squadrons, the staff was able to better incorporate them into the syllabus.

From an aircraft perspective, the last F-14 crew graduated in Class 04-03, and the Tomcat was retired from use as an adversary that October. TOPGUN acquired new F-16As, formerly designated for Pakistan, in 2003, which helped address concerns for advanced-threat simulators. From a staff perspective, TOPGUN's commanding officer structure changed in 2002, with the commanding officer, now called N7 department head, serving a slightly shorter command tour but then heading directly to command STRIKE (N5). As the decade came to an end, TOPGUN played a critical role in helping the EA-18G community stand up the Electronic Attack Weapons School (N10) at Fallon.

The 2010s: Threat Redux

The second decade of the twenty-first century in some ways resembled those surrounding the school's founding. Funds were short, assets were aging, overseas operations were largely air-to-ground, and the Navy began introducing a new high-technology fighter, the F-35C Lightning II, ironically without a gun. Like the 1970s, the Navy also faced a renewed threat from Russian long-range bombers and long-range antiship missiles. For much of the 2010s, TOPGUN focused on doing more with less and on developing new countermeasures to evolving threat tactics and hardware. Of interest is that in June 2017, a TOPGUN graduate shot down a Syrian Su-22 Fitter, marking the Navy's first air-to-air kill since Operation Desert Storm in 1991. A large part of the 2010s was also spent on integrating the new F-35C Lightning II into air wing operations and developing new tactics for the stealthy strike fighter. TOPGUN received its first F-35C students in early 2020 as part of Class 02-20 and currently has seven F-35C instructors on staff. As the school moves forward, it will continue to develop new tactics to address ever-evolving foreign adversaries, including near-peer threats presented by the Chinese J-20 and J-31, and Russian Su-57 stealth aircraft. TOPGUN is also working to become more involved in advising industry, weapons and sensor procurement, and tactics joint development.

In October 1973, TOPGUN gave all but one of its A-4s to Israel to replace aircraft losses Israel sustained in the opening days of the Yom Kippur War. Some feared this might close the School, since the Vietnam War had ended and the defense drawdown had begun. *Mersky*

Shown here are three two-seat TA-4s and an A-4F from VF-127 flying in formation. The TA-4s were used for adversary flights but also for instructor training, dignitary flights, and as a way for the RIO instructors to fly. *Mersky*

When TOPGUN lost its A-4 stable in late 1973, then commanding officer Ron "Mugs" McKeown bartered a deal with the USAF to obtain a handful of old T-38 trainers. These were quickly painted, repaired, and flying in support of the TOPGUN course. The supersonic Talon allowed instructors to simulate a MiG-21-type threat. *Grove*

One of the 242 recommendations of the Ault report called for the creation of an instrumented range for monitoring and validating missile launches and training. Cubic Corporation developed the system, known as Air Combat Maneuvering Instrumentation/ Range (ACMI/R). A pod, roughly the size of a Sidewinder missile, was fitted to the aircraft's wing and sent telemetry to the Tactical Aircrew Combat Training System (TACTS) computer. This was shown, in basic format, during the *Top Gun* movie when Kelly McGillis's character ("Charlie" Blackwood) chastised Maverick on his flying. It is now known as the Tactical Combat Training System (TCTS). *Fotodynamics*

The TOPGUN course, which had grown to five weeks by late 1974, concentrated on air-to-air combat. Using a building-block approach, students were taught 1v1 BFM and then section tactics. Here, an F-4 crew gets position on an TA-4J Skyhawk from VC-13. *Verver*

In 1974, TOPGUN took delivery of new Northrop F-5E Tiger IIs, which offered better performance than the T-38s. *Fotodynamics*

This F-5E bears the name of Jim Ruliffson, who served as a TOPGUN founding instructor and as commanding officer in 1975. Ruliffson was key in bringing the adversary oversight role to TOPGUN and in starting the F-14-oriented TOPSCOPE program. *Tailhook*

The T-38 (*first in line*) not only saved the TOPGUN course in the fall of 1973, but worked well as a supersonic aircraft representative of MiG-21-type threats. The Talons, however, became fatigued and were retired by the end of the decade. Having two adversary aircraft, though, was extremely helpful to TOPGUN in teaching tactics against likely foreign adversaries. *Tailhook*

Shown here in April 1978, this silver F-5F bears the names of instructors Steve "Smokey" Oliver and Gary "Snake" Turner (RIO). The first two-seat Tiger IIs arrived in 1975. *Grove*

This F-5F bears the name of MiG killer Willie "Spartan" Driscoll, who with Randy "Duke" Cunningham downed five MiGs during the Vietnam War. As an instructor, Driscoll revamped the surface-to-air missile threat and electronic-warfare portions of the course and further designed the students' missions to the electronic-warfare range at China Lake. Driscoll is still active with the school today, coming back for each class to lecture just prior to graduation. *Tailhook*

A VFC-13 F-5E shown during a training hop. The small Tiger IIs were difficult to see, especially from a head-on perspective and were a maintenance dream. *Fotodynamics*

An F-14 Tomcat flies over NAS Miramar.
US Navy

Despite the Tomcat's many advantages, a well-flown A-4 could often beat the F-14 in 1v1 combat. *Mersky*

The arrival of the F-14 Tomcat signaled a wholesale change in tactics for TOPGUN and ushered in maritime air superiority training. Designed as a fighter and fleet interceptor, the Tomcat replaced the F-4 and proved to be an outstanding fighter. It carried an advanced long-range radar, the AWG-9, and the long-range AIM-54 Phoenix missile. The first Tomcat crews came through TOPGUN in Class 07-76. *US Navy*

The F-14's primary role was protecting the fleet, specifically the carriers, from regimental-size raids of Soviet long-range bombers such as the Tu-95 "Bear" (*shown*), Tu-16 "Badger," and Tu-22M "Backfire" bomber. The idea was to kill the archer (the bomber) before it could launch its quiver (cruise missile). *US Navy Historical Center*

The Tomcat's main weapon was its long-range AIM-54 Phoenix missile. The Tomcat carried up to six Phoenix, which had a published range of over 118 miles. When not carrying Phoenix, the Tomcat carried a mix of AIM-7 Sparrow and AIM-9 Sidewinder missiles, and could use its 20 mm cannon. *US Navy*

Shown here in February 1979, this A-4E is painted in a gray/blue camouflage. TOPGUN operated a mixed adversary unit of T-38s, F-5s, and A-4s for a period from 1975 to 1979. *Grove*

The need to teach F-14 crews on maritime air superiority tactics fostered the development of TOPSCOPE, which ran from 1976 to 1980. The course was largely for RIOs, but pilots did attend. In 1981, TOPSCOPE was folded into a longer combined Power Projection course for one year, then split into the F-14 FRS and a traveling road show of lectures called Fleet Air Superiority Training (FAST). *Finta*

The F-14 made its initial deployment in 1974 aboard USS *Enterprise* (CVN-65). It remains the fighter most associated with TOPGUN. Here, three VF-41 "Black Aces" fly in formation in the late 1990s. *Fotodynamics*

Some A-4s, such as the Modex 554 shown here in January 1976, wore a plain low-visibility gray scheme. TOPGUN experimented with various camouflage patterns during the mid-1970s. *Grove*

Shown here is the F-5 of Cdr. Jerry Unruh, TOPGUN's commanding officer from 1978 to 1979. Unruh was a former F-8 pilot and was involved in the Navy's first MiG engagement in 1965, although no kills resulted. *Fotodynamics*

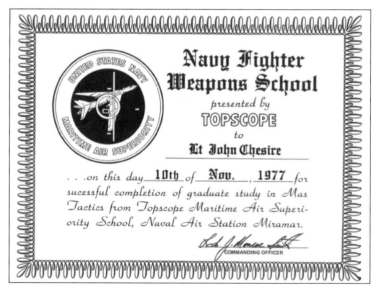

Tomcat pilot John Chesire attended TOPGUN in Class 01-72 and graduated TOPSCOPE in November 1977. *Chesire*

A TOPGUN F-5F takes off at NAS Miramar in February 1979. The two-seat F-5F allowed RIO instructors to fly during training missions against students. TOPGUN usually had four to five RIOs on staff at any given time. *Grove*

When TOPGUN retired its F-5s in 1987, several adversary squadrons, including VF-127, added the type and took up flying it against the fleet. TOPGUN's Adversary instructor course commenced in 1975 and continued to flourish during the 1980s and even today. *Mersky*

This image of an F-5E and an F-5F highlights the different paint schemes used on TOPGUN's adversary aircraft. *Mersky*

The F-5E proved an excellent adversary aircraft and is still in use today. Shown here are Tiger IIs from VF-43. *Mersky*

Two A-4 Skyhawks head into a shallow right turn during maneuvers. Both are TOPGUN jets from the 1977–1979 period. As the decade wound down, TOPGUN began looking for a new adversary aircraft, since the MiG-17 and MiG-21 were no longer the predominant threat on the world stage. *Verver*

An F-14A and F-8 Crusader fly alongside two A-4s in August 1979. This image highlights the vast size difference between the Tomcat and the Skyhawk. *Verver*

A group of students in Class 07-76 debrief following a flight. Notice the dark-blue flight suit worn by the instructor leading the discussion. These were worn from 1973 until the early 1980s. *US Navy*

Some of the maritime air superiority lectures formerly associated with TOPSCOPE were pushed down into VF-124 "Gunfighters," the F-14 FRS, while others became part of TOPGUN's FAST program. *US Navy*

CHAPTER 4
TOPGUN Today

Based at NAS Fallon, today's TOPGUN conducts three twelve-week courses per year, with each consisting of three programs: the SFTI course, AIC course, and Adversary course. Each SFTI course consists of nine crews, designated as TG-1, -2, -3P, -4W, etc., of F/A-18E/F Super Hornet crews, as well as Marine Corps F/A-18C/D Legacy Hornet crews. At least three of the SFTI course attendees are weapons system officers (WSOs) from the two-scat Navy F/A-18F community or the Marines F/A-18D community.

The TOPGUN course is divided into four phases: Basic Fighter Maneuvering (BFM), Air-to-Surface, Section, and Division. Each phase runs between three and three and a half weeks except for Air-to-Surface, which is two weeks. All phases are conducted at NAS Fallon except the BFM phase, which rotates through fleet training areas such as Lemoore, Oceana, and Miramar, with occasional detachments (dets) to Pensacola or Key West. This rotation gives the staff an opportunity to interact with the fleet squadrons, allowing instructors to give guest lectures to squadrons and guest flights (Rush Rides) to prospective students. Moreover, the BFM det allows the students to fly 1v1 (one aircraft versus a single adversary) sorties at sea level, where they are more likely to operate on deployment and can further maximize the performance of their jets.

Instruction comes through lectures, labs, flights, and briefing and debriefing. Lectures discuss topics such as "Blue" (friendly) hardware (APG-79 radar, AIM-9 missiles, and laser-guided munitions), "Red" threat systems (pilots and weapons), and tactics. Even with extensive and detailed lectures, the bulk of the training is imparted through the postmission debriefs. It is here that the students are taught the art of debriefing to instruct. Each flight is critiqued by the flight members, including the participating AICs and adversary aircraft crews, with TOPGUN instructors providing comments and critiquing the students' debriefs. Learning to properly debrief is a key skill that all TOPGUN graduates must have to effectively draw out and pass along the lessons learned from each training flight.

Adversary and AIC students join the course just after the SFTI students complete the BFM phase, which typically is three to three and a half weeks into the course. Adversary and AIC students receive the same lectures as the SFTI students, plus a few additional lectures tailored to their specific needs. Adversary students conduct an abbreviated BFM phase while the SFTI students complete Air-to-Surface, then start leading Red air events for multiplane section and division flights. AIC students typically come into the fold to control section and division events, and all three courses graduate together, with each student receiving the appropriate patch signifying their successful completion of the course.

TOPGUN also offers other programs, including its three-day Senior Officer Course (SOC) and a Re-Blue event, held each fall, which invites all patch wearers back to Fallon for a short three-day update on tactics. TOPGUN also provides subject matter lectures to fleet squadrons during its BFM dets, which helps gives the school much-valued time with the fleet squadrons, something that has been less frequent since TOPGUN departed Miramar for Fallon in 1996. The school patches roughly thirty-three to thirty-six pilots and WSOs, twelve AICs, and twelve adversary instructors per year.

TOPGUN is now stronger than ever and is widely accepted as the center of excellence for fighter tactics training. Throughout its long history, this culture has developed through the dedication of its instructor staff. Traditions such as the Murder Board, which thoroughly vets new instructor's lectures, and the Standardization Board, which oversees the instructor training and the development of new tactics, work to ensure that TOPGUN instructors are the best of the best and that the lessons passed along by its instructors are sound.

TOPGUN's current staff stands at roughly thirty-five instructors, the majority of whom are Navy lieutenants or Marine Corps captains. These instructors, each of whom are well-qualified subject matter experts (SMEs) in topics such as radar, missile systems, threat aircraft, and tactics, go through an intense program of training, both in flying and in their SME topic areas. Before any instructor can fly against a TOPGUN class student, he or she must work through a rigorous Instructor under Training (IUT) program, which qualifies them to teach and fly "red air" and in the course's various phases.

Before an instructor can speak on behalf of TOPGUN, whether to the Navy or a class, the instructor must go through a lengthy preboard process of researching and developing a lecture, culminating in a final Murder Board before all instructors. Murder Boards require prospective instructors to fluidly present their lecture, without notes, and without consulting their slides, at an expert level. This demanding IUT and Murder Board process, coupled with the staff's willingness to call one another when someone does not meet the school's standards, has ensured a culture of excellence that has continued since TOPGUN's founding.

When TOPSCOPE ended in 1980, its contents were largely pushed into an expanded Power Projection course syllabus. After a year, several of the maritime air superiority lectures were removed from the course and placed into what was known as FAST—Fleet Air Superiority Training—and given to fleet units as a detachment. *US Navy*

As the F-4 was retired, the Tomcat became the main Navy fighter. Most Navy students coming through the course in the early 1980s flew the F-14, while Marine students flew the F-4 Phantom. *Fotodynamics*

In the late 1970s, TOPGUN began sending its students to fly against captured MiGs at Tonopah. Part of the secretive 4477th Squadron "Red Eagles," the MiGs were a collection of MiG-17s, MiG-21s, and MiG-23s. *USAF*

The A-4E Skyhawk remained a primary adversary aircraft for TOPGUN throughout the 1980s but was less and less representative of foreign threats. *Grove*

A camouflaged F-5E sits by a hangar at Miramar. *Fotodynamics*

TOPGUN considered the proposed Northrop F-20 as a replacement for the F-5E. The Tigershark featured an enhanced engine that greatly improved overall performance and a modern avionics suite, including a multimode APG-67 radar. *Northrop*

Two Soviet fourth-generation fighters appeared in the 1980s, causing TOPGUN to reevaluate its tactics against highly maneuverable fighters employing all-aspect missiles. The MiG-29 Fulcrum, *shown here*, and the Su-27 Flanker presented serious challenges to US air superiority. *US Navy*

The F-15C operated by the USAF represented the pinnacle of air superiority aircraft. In the early 1980s, TOPGUN began an exchange program with the USAF Weapons School F-15 Division, whereby an Eagle driver joined the TOPGUN staff for a three-year tour. *Fotodynamics*

Initially, F-5 instructor training was handled by the USAF but later was done internally by TOPGUN staff. *Fotodynamics*

TOPGUN instructors put hundreds of hours of preparation into each lecture, refining their presentations both in content and style. Instructors must pass a demanding Murder Board process before they can speak on behalf of TOPGUN. In a Murder Board, the lecture is given to all instructors, who must vote yes, or no, as to whether the speaker is ready. *Baranek*

Former Soviet air force MiG-25 pilot Victor Belenko defected from the Soviet Union in 1976 and made several visits to TOPGUN to lecture instructors and meet with students. *Baranek*

The first USAF F-15 exchange officer was F-15C pilot Mike "Boa" Straight (*left*), shown here with Marine TOPGUN instructor Terry "Circus" McGuire. Straight was instrumental in helping TOPGUN prepare for the arrival of the single-seat F/A-18. The Eagle and the Hornet, made by McDonnell Douglas, were both single-seat platforms and required all radar work to be performed by the pilot. *Baranek*

In addition to the exchange instructor, TOPGUN and the USAF Weapons School F-15 Division frequently met to discuss tactics and fly against one another. *Baranek*

The A-4 Skyhawk and F-5 Tiger II were TOPGUN's sole adversary aircraft from 1980 to 1987. *Baranek*

Shown here are three F-5s in a variety of paint schemes. TOPGUN developed different camouflage patterns to make their adversary aircraft harder to see and to better reflect the paint schemes used by US foreign adversaries. *Baranek*

The arrival of the Hornet in the mid-1980s, required the creation of new lectures and flights suited to the new aircraft. The Hornet proved an excellent fighter even in the hands of a relatively inexperienced pilot. *Mersky*

TOPGUN's F-5s were aging by the mid-1980s and were nearing the end of their service life. The NFWS' Tiger IIs were fatigue leaders of all F-5s worldwide. *Baranek*

A Hornet from VMFA-323 escorts a Soviet Tupolev Tu-16 Badger during a 1985–86 deployment. The Hornets were both a fighter and attack platform. TOPGUN incorporated a peacetime escort mission into their teachings as a result of the realities of air operations in the Mediterranean. *NAM*

Implemented in the mid-1970s, TOPGUN's instructors made an annual trek to Yuma or El Centro for an instructor-only guns detachment. The F-5 shown here displays soot near its gun barrel after a gun det in Key West, Florida. The gun Dets ended in the mid- to late-1980s. *Baranek*

Two TOPGUN F-5s painted black and the camera-equipped Lear Jet used for much of the *Top Gun* movie photography. *Baranek*

TOPGUN instructors Bob "Rat" Willard and Dave "Bio" Baranek stand by one of the movie's black "MiG-28s." *Baranek*

Thanks to the 1986 *Top Gun* movie, the NFWS became a household name, and its patch, featured on this instructor's helmet, gained instant worldwide recognition. *Baranek*

Although the school has switched between "Top Gun" and "TOPGUN," the official designation is one word, all caps—TOPGUN. *Baranek*

TOPGUN replaced its F-5s with new F-16Ns in 1987. The sleek, highly maneuverable Vipers had an uprated engine and had been stripped of their gun and wing pylons, making them extremely light. *Baranek*

The NFWS said goodbye to its F-5s in September 1987. The Tiger IIs had served the school well during their thirteen-year service. *Nickell*

A VF-114 "Aardvark" F-14 Tomcat and a VFC-13 A-4 Skyhawk doing battle. *Verver*

TOPGUN often took a small number of planes and instructors to Nellis to fly with the USAF. Unlike USAF F-15 Division instructors, TOPGUN's instructors flew adversary only against the students ("red air"), while USAF instructors flew with the students ("blue air"). *Verver*

Flown properly, the F-5 could mimic the MiG-23's flight characteristics. Lacking radar, it relied on ground control for intercepts. *Baranek*

The second F-16N arrived at TOPGUN in the late summer of 1987. The Viper could effectively simulate the MiG-17, MiG-21, MiG-23, and MiG-29, depending on how the pilot used afterburner and self-limited turning. *Baranek*

As the 1980s ended, the Tomcat still dominated fleet fighter squadrons and dictated the all-air-to-air syllabus for the TOPGUN course. *US Navy*

TOPGUN's F-5s were painted black and used as the fictitious "MiG-28" for the filming of the *Top Gun* movie. *Fotodynamics*

Dogfighting remained the focus of TOPGUN's academics and flights until early 1994, when air-to-ground employment was reincorporated into the syllabus. Here a Tomcat maneuvers against an F-16N. *Fotodynamics*

When TOPGUN reorganized adversary training in 1975, the Navy created dedicated adversary squadrons, including VF-127 Cyclons, that flew the F-5. TOPGUN holds an Adversary Instructor Course as part of each TOPGUN class. Adversary students typically start during the third week of the course after the SFTI students return from BFM Det. Air Intercept Control (AIC) students also begin class at this point. *Fotodynamics*

CHAPTER 5

The Aircraft of TOPGUN

A-4 Skyhawk

TOPGUN's first adversary aircraft was the McDonnell Douglas A-4 Skyhawk, specifically the two-seat TA-4J. TOPGUN had no aircraft of its own beyond the F-4 Phantoms flown by VF-121, so it borrowed adversary aircraft from VF-126 "Bandits," an instrument-training squadron co-located at NAS Miramar. This arrangement continued into 1971, when the school gained access to a small number of A-4Es. The Skyhawk proved an excellent representation of the Mikoyan-Gurevich MiG-17 Fresco flown by the North Vietnamese in the skies over Southeast Asia. The A-4 was highly maneuverable and flew well at slow speeds.

TOPGUN received its own A-4E/F Skyhawks in 1972, just prior to becoming its own independent command. TOPGUN flew these without wing pylons and removed the 20 mm cannon, modifications that reduced weight and drag and increased performance. The two-seater versions were used for training new instructors, flying visiting dignitaries, and flying instructor RIOs. TOPGUN continued to fly A-4s into the early 1990s, retiring the aircraft in May 1994. The final variant was the A-4M, which was acquired from the Marine Corps in the early 1992–1993 period. A well-flown A-4 was a good match for the F-14 Tomcat and F/A-18 Hornet.

T-38A/B Talon

In October 1973, TOPGUN sustained a serious setback when all but one of its Skyhawks were commandeered and given to the Israelis, who had sustained heavy losses in the 1973 Arab-Israeli (Yom Kippur) War. The transfer left TOPGUN with only one aircraft for its course, causing some to worry that the school might be shut down. In a radical move by Skipper Ron "Mugs" McKeown, a deal was brokered for TOPGUN to obtain a handful of discarded USAF T-38A/B Talons. The supersonic Talons proved a solid representation of the Soviet-built MiG-21 Fishbed, which was

still the primary opponent of Western air forces around the world. The school flew the T-38s until the late 1970s.

F-5E/F Tiger II

Even though the Talons provided a good MiG-21 stand-in, TOPGUN wanted more, and in mid-1974 it began searching for a new adversary aircraft. By late 1974, the Northrop F-5E/F Tiger II arrived. A sleek, maneuverable, and supersonic fighter that could be flown to mimic the MiG-21, the Tiger IIs provided adversary until 1987, when they were replaced by the F-16N. The F-5E/F was used during the filming of the movie *Top Gun*, serving as the fictitious "MiG-28" fighter. These were painted black to make them appear more sinister.

F-16N Viper

Seeking to better replicate fourth-generation threats such as the Soviet MiG-29 Fulcrum and Su-27 Flanker, TOPGUN began looking for a new adversary aircraft in the early 1980s, ultimately selecting the F-16N, a hybrid variant combining a standard small-inlet F-16C/D Block 30 with the powerful General Electric F110-GE-100 engine and carrying the F-16A/B's APG-66 radar. The F-16N had no cannon or self-protect jamming system and no wing pylons but did carry a radar-warning receiver and ALE-40 chaff/flare dispenser.

The Mach 2+, 9-G capable Viper, as it was called at TOPGUN, was a favorite of the staff and truly allowed instructors to represent the full gambit of air threats faced by US aircrew. The Viper could be flown to represent the older MiG-23 or the latest MiG-29/Su-27. The first F-16Ns arrived in 1987. Two two-seat TF-16Ns were also acquired. The aircraft were usually flown during the more advanced training, while the A-4 Skyhawks were flown during the initial 1v1 BFM flights. Over time, however, the high-g maneuvering lead to the development of stress cracks in the Vipers' tails. Eventually the school was forced to give up the Vipers, which many felt was a significant loss both to the course and the fleet.

F-14A Tomcat

In August 1991, TOPGUN received its first F-14A Tomcats. At the time, the Tomcat was the fleet's primary fighter and constituted roughly 50 percent of any given TOPGUN student class. The Tomcats allowed visiting East Coast students and those from Japan to use TOPGUN's jets, rather than bring their own. They also allowed instructors to fly what was called "blue air" with the students, which meant the instructors flew as part of the instructional mission rather than as adversary. Additionally, the Tomcats allowed instructors to remain current while serving as TOPGUN staff. Some F-14s were also used as adversary, but the use of Tomcats against other Tomcats created dissimilar air combat training (DACT) issues. Unfortunately, the Tomcats were older models and were frequently in maintenance. Tomcat readiness suffered significantly, and even those that were able to fly often lacked a working radar. TOPGUN (and later NSAWC) continued to maintain a small fleet of F-14s (roughly six to seven) through the first few years of the twenty-first century, until the final F-14 students came through the school in 2003 as part of Class 04-03. Tomcats were retired from fleet usage in 2006.

F/A-18 Hornet

TOPGUN obtained a small number of F/A-18 Hornets beginning in September 1994. Eventually, the school would have about twenty single-seat F/A-18As and two dual-seat F/A-18Bs. These Hornets were obtained from a Lemoore-based Hornet squadron transitioning to the newer F/A-18C. Early Hornets were older-lot aircraft and suffered from maintenance issues, leading to availability problems that lasted into the twenty-first century. TOPGUN and later NSAWC continued to fly the F/A-18A/B models well into this century, when they were replaced by newer C/D models. NSAWC (predecessor to the current NAWDC) obtained a number of F/A-18C/Ds in the first few years of this century for adversary and "blue air" training flights. As has been the case for most of TOPGUN's history, many of these models were older aircraft that were not fleet representative.

F-16A/B Falcon

In 2001, TOPGUN obtained a small number of F-16A/B Falcons that had been destined for Pakistan but had been canceled for political reasons. While not as sleek as the F-16Ns, the F-16Ns brought back a true DACT capability that had been lacking since the 1995 departure of the F-16Ns. These Falcons are still in use at NAWDC, the entity that now oversees TOPGUN. NAWDC and TOPGUN are currently evaluating new adversary alternatives, which include new Block 70 F-16s. This model is based on the advanced F-16V configuration and features the APG-83 AESA radar, new displays and avionics, and structural upgrades to extend the aircraft's service life by more than 50 percent beyond that of previous F-16 production aircraft.

F/A-18E/F Super Hornet

NSAWC received its first Super Hornets in 2008, which became available both for TOPGUN (N7) and Air Wing Training/Strike (N5). TOPGUN currently operates a fleet of single-seat model E and two-seat model F Super Hornets, most of which are early-lot production aircraft; none are recent-lot Block II models. The Super Hornets are used for "blue air" flights, adversary training, instructor training, and tactics evaluation and development (TE&D) flights.

Camouflage and Markings

Camouflage was used beginning in the mid-1970s to make the adversary aircraft more difficult to see during dogfights. Colorful patterns were experimented with over the years, but most were multicolored/tricolored variants of browns, blues, and desert colors. During the 1990s, one F-14 and an F/A-18 were painted black. The camouflage made the already small A-4 and F-5 extremely difficult to see against earth or desert backgrounds and in later years (post-1994) also helped students distinguish between friendly aircraft (from the course) and adversary.

During the time at Miramar, TOPGUN's jets were marked rather simplistically, featuring a large number on the nose or tail fin (or both) and a TOPGUN patch on the tail fin. When the school relocated to Fallon and became a department within NSAWC, the jets, which then belonged to NSAWC, were given new tail markings featuring a small TOPGUN patch within a lightning bolt, the latter being a brand of STRIKE.

The F-14 Tomcat and F/A-18 Hornet entered the 1990s as the Navy's combined fighter force. TOPGUN often taught mixed-section tactics, where each aircraft could utilize the unique advantages of its radar. Mixed section work was introduced by the USAF F-15 Weapons Division Exchange Officer during the early 1980s, since the Eagles had experience working with the F-16 Falcon. *US Navy*

A-4 Skyhawks remained a potent adversary aircraft even into the early 1990s. Some A-4s were given Marine Corps markings, highlighting the Marines' contributions to the School. Typically 4-5 Marines served on staff, including at least one Air Intercept Controller (AIC). *Fotodynamics*

Several A-4Fs seen in April–May 1992, sporting the various camouflage patterns used by TOPGUN. *Verver*

TOPGUN took possession of three F-14As in August 1991, and eventually maintained a stable of four to six Tomcats. The Tomcats were retired at TOPGUN/NSAWC in the fall of 2003. *Fotodynamics*

Three TOPGUN adversary aircraft and an F/A-18A Hornet from VFC-13 are shown here. VFC-12 and VFC-13 assumed much of TOPGUN's adversary responsibilities post-1993. *Denneny*

A NFWS F-14 and F/A-18 are shown here in light-blue camouflage. These aircraft were flown as "red air" (adversary) and "blue air" (friendly) aircraft. Flying "blue air" with the students provides additional training opportunities for the instructors and allows them to better demonstrate the proper way to brief, execute the mission, and debrief. *Twomey*

An F-14A banks hard left and shows off its colorful blue tritone camouflage. *Twomey*

TOPGUN flew the A-4, F-5, and F-16N together for a very short period in 1987, until the instructors became certified to fly the Viper and sufficient numbers of the F-16N were available. *Mersky*

Operation Desert Storm was largely an Air Force air operation. The Navy played a small role in air-to-air engagements and largely provided suppression of enemy air defenses (SEAD) and support for troops on the ground. *USAF*

Prior to the implementation of SFTI in 1995, TOPGUN students came to the school from their squadrons, along with two aircraft and maintainers, and returned upon completion of the course. Most graduates were used as training officers, but not all. *Llinares*

The A-4Ms were obtained from the Marine Corps in the early 1990s and retired from TOPGUN in May 1994. *Top, Fotodynamics; bottom, Grove*

The fatigue issues eventually forced TOPGUN to retire its F-16Ns in 1995. The loss of the Vipers was a huge blow to the School's prestige and its ability to simulate Fourth Generation threats. *Mersky*

TOPGUN relocated to NAS Fallon in mid-1996 and became a department within the Naval Strike and Air Warfare Center (NSAWC). The new tail markings combined TOPGUN's patch and Strike's signature lightning bolt. *Fotodynamics*

TOPGUN instructors, as with all NSAWC officers, had to wear the NSWC triangle after the merger into NSAWC. *Author*

Top and above: Some of the F-16Ns had very distinct camouflage patterns, such as these two Vipers wearing Marine Corps markings. *Fotodynamics (top); Mersky (above)*

In 1992, TOPGUN moved into its new building at NAS Miramar (shown here under construction) only to turn it over to the Marines when the school relocated to Fallon in 1996. *Denneny*

The new facility at Fallon was patterned after the 1992 building. Here, an NSAWC F/A-18 flies over the Fleet Training Building (FTB) in Fallon, where TOPGUN is currently located. *Fotodynamics*

VFC-13 relocated to NAS Fallon and provided adversary support for TOPGUN, Strike air wing training, and fleet squadrons going through the Fleet Fighter Air Combat Readiness Program (FFARP) and Strike Fighter Advanced Readiness Program (SFARP). *Fotodynamics*

A line of NSAWC Tomcats at NAS Fallon. In 2015, NSAWC was renamed the Naval Air Warfare Development Center (NAWDC). *Fotodynamics*

F-14s were still used as adversary in the early 2000s for certain student flights. Here two Tomcats maneuver against one another. *Fotodynamics*

TOPGUN's F-14As were older models and were prone to maintenance issues, causing many flight cancellations. *Grove*

The "Bombcat's" air-to-ground capability gave the Tomcat new life after the end of the Cold War. *US Navy*

Compliance with the Strike Fighter Weapons and Tactics (SFWT) training syllabus is handled by SFTIs from a coastal weapons school. Shown here are patches for Strike Fighter Weapons School, Pacific, and Atlantic. The weapons school SFTIs administer "check rides" for squadron aircrews going through their Strike Fighter Weapons and Training (SFWT) syllabus, which qualifies crews to fly Combat Wing, Combat Section Lead, and Combat Division Lead. They also provide lectures to fleet squadrons and administer the Strike Fighter Advanced Readiness Program (SFARP) for squadrons as they prepare to deploy. *Author*

In 2003, NSAWC acquired approximately fourteen F-16A/B Falcons originally destined for Pakistan but canceled. The Falcons greatly enhanced TOPGUN's ability to represent the latest threats faced by aircrews. *Hunter*

From 1998 through 2003, TOPGUN ran two separate courses: a five-week all-Marine course and a ten-week all-Navy course. *Fotodynamics*

The first F/A-18F Super Hornet crew attended Class 05-01. The first F/A-18 Super Hornet arrived at Fallon in 2008. *Hunter*

F-14 pilot and RIO instructors played a significant role in developing the early crew coordination recommendations for the new two-seat F/A-18F. *Fotodynamics*

VFC-12 "Fighting Omars" out of NAS Oceana provided SFARP training for East Coast squadrons during early air wing workups. *US Navy*

Operations Enduring Freedom (Afghanistan) and Iraqi Freedom (Iraq) were almost exclusively air-to-ground ventures. As a result, TOPGUN worked to incorporate more fleet-representative training missions into its syllabus. *US Navy*

A line of NSAWC F/A-18A-D Hornets are shown here at Fallon being prepared for a mission. *Neil Pearson*

The final F-14 students came through TOPGUN in 2003, Class 04-03. The graduates of this class were sent to the east coast strike fighter weapons school, called SFWSL, and they became the F-14 squadron training officers for the final Tomcat squadrons. *US Navy*

The Tomcat was finally retired from Navy service in 2006, ending a long career with the military branch. *US Navy*

For a brief period during the first few years of this century, TOPGUN operated the F-16A/B, F-14A, and F/A-18 Hornet. *Fotodynamics*

Two NSAWC F-16s in formation over the desert. The F-16A/B has proven extremely valuable at replicating modern foreign threats, but TOPGUN and NAWDC are working to obtain new adversary aircraft, hopefully the new F-16V. Although obtained in 2002, they have undergone upgrades to remain viable. *Fotodynamics*

TOPGUN works with the USAF F-22 squadrons to give its instructors and students exposure to fifth-generation aircraft threats and with EA-18G Growler squadrons to coordinate electronic warfare (EW). A handful of TOPGUN instructors also flew the F-22 with USAF squadrons, providing a direct link back to TOPGUN. *US Navy*

Even with the Falcons, the Hornet and Super Hornet remain the predominate aircraft at NSAWC/NAWDC. Currently at least three of the four tactical squadrons in the carrier air wing are Super Hornets. Usually an air wing has three single-seat squadrons of either F/A-18C or F/A-18E aircraft and a single squadron of two-seat F/A-18F. The Navy retired its last Legacy Hornet in 2019, and will soon deploy the new F-35C. Marine Corps Hornet squadrons will continue to deploy with air wings until they fully transition to the F-35C. *Fotodynamics*

The F-14 is seen here with an F-16 and F/A-18. *Fotodynamics*

Shown here is a camouflaged F/A-18C fighting a student flying an F/A-18F. TOPGUN utilizes a building block approach to teach advanced air combat tactics and begins each class with a week of Basic Combat Maneuvering (BFM) to hone the students' skills. It then works through air-to-surface, section, and division phases, each building on the prior lessons. *Fotodynamics*

A blue tricolored F-16A prepares for a mission at NSAWC. *Author*

The Block II Super Hornet introduced the Joint Helmet Mounted Cuing System (JHMCS), which could be used with the high off-bore site (HOBS) AIM-9X Sidewinder and various targeting sensors. *Hunter and US Navy*

Four NSAWC Falcons enter a shallow right bank. *Fotodynamics*

The VFC-111 "Sundowners" located at NAS Key West provide adversary support for East Coast squadrons and TOPGUN students who come through on BFM detachment. *Fotodynamics*

A TOPGUN student completes a systems check before takeoff in an F/A-18C. *US Navy*

TOPGUN obtained an F-16 simulator and since 2008–2009 has conducted its own instructor F-16A training. *Author*

An NSAWC F/A-18 is shown in blue multi-tone camouflage. *Fotodynamics*

Two Super Hornets blast through a valley at Fallon during an exercise. *Hunter*

Other communities have adopted TOPGUN's WTI
approach to their respective weapons schools. The P-3
Orion community created a weapons school located at
NAS Jacksonville, Florida, patterned after TOPGUN, but
for maritime warfare. *Author*

Under SFTI, the TOPGUN graduate serves a three-year training tour either at TOPGUN, an FRS, a weapons school, Strike, or a VX squadron before returning to the fleet as squadron training officer. *Llinares*

Navy tactical air power played a huge role in air operations over Afghanistan, which ran from 2001 into the 2010s, and lessons learned were incorporated into SFTI classes. *US Navy*

The F/A-18E/F Super Hornet has been the primary tactical Navy aircraft since 2006, allowing TOPGUN to concentrate on it and the Legacy Hornet. *Llinares*

The Su-35 "Flanker-E," a derivative of the Su-27, first appeared in 2008. The most capable fighter in the Russian arsenal, it features a redesigned cockpit and weapons-control system and has thrust-vectoring engines in place of canards. *Mladenov*

A close-up of a pilot preparing for a mission at Fallon. *Hunter*

Students coming to TOPGUN's SFTI course are provided with fleet-representative aircraft by the East and West Coast strike fighter wings at Lemoore and Oceana. This alleviated the need under the old Power Projection course conscript for each squadron to send two aircraft and maintainers to support a squadron aircrew. *Llinares*

An excellent profile of an NSAWC F-16A in a light-blue camouflage pattern. *Hunter*

The FTB at NAS Fallon is where TOPGUN instructors work each day. This hallway features the graduation photos of all classes, as well as the original dedication plaque from the new TOPGUN building in Miramar. *NSAWC*

The Frank Ault Auditorium, named in 2007, is where TOPGUN holds its class opening ceremony as well as its graduation ceremony and hosts various MiG-killer lectures. *NSAWC*

The first Phase of the TOPGUN SFTI course is Basic Fighter Maneuvering (BFM), where students are taught how to best employ their aircraft versus a single adversary. A 1v1 BFM brief typically takes about an hour, the flight about 0.5–0.8, and the debrief about two hours. *Hunter*

The two-seat F-16B gives weapons system officers (WSOs; formerly called RIOs) the opportunity to fly training missions against students. *Hunter*

Former TOPGUN instructor David "Chip" Berke not only flew the F-22 with the USAF but also commanded the first F-35 training squadron, VMFAT-501 "Warlords," at Eglin AFB. Berke's staff had several TOPGUN patch wearers, who worked to develop the early tactics for the F-35 and passed on that information back to the Schoolhouse, and to VFA-101 "Ghost Riders," the Navy's initial F-35C FRS. *US Navy*

TOPGUN began working to integrate the F-35 into Navy air wings through a series of test-and-evaluation cooperatives with VMFAT-501 "Warlords" and VFA-101 "Grim Reapers," beginning in 2014 and continuing even today. *US Navy*

The Super Hornet excels at air-to-air and air-to-ground and has assumed many of the missions of the F-14 Tomcat, including Forward Air Control–Airborne (FAC-A) and reconnaissance. *Hunter*

The F-16A/B continues to provide a suitable simulator for most foreign threats. *Hunter*

By 2006, all tactical strike aircraft in the carrier were some version of the F/A-18A/C Hornet or F/A-18E/F Super Hornet, making TOPGUN's job to devise tactics somewhat easier, since all squadrons operated a similar aircraft. *US Navy*

NSAWC's F-16A/Bs support both the TOPGUN course and air wing events. At times, TOPGUN instructors fly "red air" adversary for Air Wing Fallon. *US Navy*

In the Section phase of the SFTI syllabus, TOPGUN works to impart section tactics skills to students, essentially teaching them how to employ the Hornet in a two-ship formation. *Fotodynamics*

TOPGUN's instructors occasionally fly with USAF F-22 Raptors to develop tactics against fifth-generation fighters. *US Navy*

TOPGUN instructors fly the F-16A as "red air," providing realistic adversary presentations for students. *Hunter*

Five F/A-18 Hornets of various models await launch at NAS Fallon in support of an NSAWC event. *US Navy*

This light-blue camouflage pattern simulates a Russian Su-27 color scheme. *Hunter*

Lt. Cdr. Michael "M.O.B." Tremel, a graduate of Class 02-11 and former TOPGUN instructor, scored an Su-22 Fitter kill over Syria, using an AMRAAM, registering the first Super Hornet kill. *US Navy*

A desert-camouflaged F-16A sits next to a low-visibility gray Navy and Marine Corps fleet jet waiting to take off for a TOPGUN mission. *Hunter*

An NSAWC F/A-18F and F-16B fly over the ranges of Fallon in this 2016 photo. *Hunter*

Two F/A-18 Hornets release flares in this image taken at NAS Fallon. *Fotodynamics*

The first F-35C students attended SFTI Class 02-20 beginning in January 2020. There are currently seven F-35C instructors on the TOPGUN staff. *US Navy*

The A-4 Skyhawk, a Vietnam-era light attack aircraft, was a delta-winged, single turbojet engine subsonic aircraft capable of roughly 690 mph. *Mersky*

An F/A-18A Hornet attached to the NFWS conducts a flight during a training mission in the 1990s. *US Navy*

The Navy and Marine Corps obtained a small number of Israel Aircraft Industries Kfir, which was a Mach 2.0 aircraft based on the French Dassault Mirage 5. The Navy flew these from 1985 to 1989, with VF-43 at Oceana to represent the MiG-23. The Marines flew them with VMFA-401. *Mersky*

TOPGUN's adversary aircraft circa 1991: two F-16Ns and two A-4s. *Verver*

VX-9 Vampires, a test-and-evaluation squadron based at China Lake, is one of five destinations for TOPGUN's SFTIs upon graduation. *Shemley*

A line of F-16s prepare for a night mission at Fallon. *Fotodynamics*

One of the special black schemes used in the 1990s on an F/A-18B. *Fotodynamics*

The A-4M was the final Skyhawk variant flown by TOPGUN. *Fotodynamics*

A sampling of the various camouflage schemes flown by TOPGUN. *Fotodynamics*

Three colorful adversary aircraft are shown here: NSAWC F/A-18A, VMFT-401 F-5E, and VFC-13 F-5E (*top to bottom*). *Fotodynamics*

A close-up of VFC-13's tiger paint scheme. The "Saints" supported NAWDC's TOPGUN and STRIKE training and provide SFARP for West Coast fleet squadrons. *Fotodynamics*

TOPGUN taught night tactics at various times in the mid-1980s through the mid-1990s, and then again circa 2003–2006. *Llinares*

VFC-13 currently flies F/-5E/Fs and uses a variety of camouflage patterns to make the already small jet even more difficult to see visually. *Ramos*

Adversary aircraft currently flown by TOPGUN: the F-16B Falcon and F/A-18 Hornet. *Ramos*

Two F-5s are shown here: a VFC-13 F-5F (*foreground*) and a VFC-111 F-5E (*background*). *Fotodynamics*

NAWDC and TOPGUN continue to use creative camouflage patterns
to simulate foreign-threat aircraft. *Fotodynamics*

The F-14 Tomcat was the Navy's frontline fighter from 1972 through the early
1990s, when it picked up an air-to-ground role and became a strike fighter
alongside the Hornet. *US Navy*

The Northrop F-5E/F was a lightweight day fighter that proved to be a
near-perfect simulation for the MiG-21. It was used at TOPGUN from mid-1974
through September 1987. *Mersky*

TOPGUN SFTI students spend one week on a dedicated BFM detachment held at a coastal location (Oceana, Miramar, Key West, or Beaufort) and then learn section and division tactics at Fallon. *Fotodynamics*

The Tomcat proved to be a much-better fighter than the F-4 Phantom II it replaced, outperforming the F-4 in turns, acceleration, and slow-speed operations. *Fotodynamics*

Designated as an adversary squadron in 1973, VF-43 "Challengers" was based at Oceana and supported Atlantic fleet fighter squadrons. They flew the A-4F/J and TA-4F/J Skyhawk, T-38A Talon, F-16N Viper, and F-21A Kfir. *Mersky*

An F-16N is shown on the Miramar flight line as an F-14 Tomcat approaches for landing. *National Archives*

Pilots loved flying the F-16N. Some aircrew would score a "hat trick" by flying the Viper, Skyhawk, and Hornet or Tomcat all in a single day. *Mersky*

The "black" F/A-18B Hornet shown here in TOPGUN markings ca. 1994–1996. *Twomey*

Paramount painted some of the TOPGUN F-5s black to cast a more sinister appearance on their fictitious "MiG-28." This is a VFC-13 Tiger II emulating that scheme. *Ramos*

This F-16Ns was given a three-tone blue camouflage to simulate the Su-27 Flanker. *Fotodynamics*

Dispute its similarity to the T-38A, the F-5E was a much-improved aircraft that was described as easy to fly and easy to maintain. *Mersky*

This T-38B was one of the aircraft obtained by Cdr. "Mugs" McKeown in the fall of 1973, when the school's Skyhawks were transferred to the Israelis. *Fotodynamics*

This image highlights the various adversary aircraft flown by VF-126. *From top to bottom*: F-16N, F-5E, A-4, and TA-4, followed by a T-2 Buckeye. *National Archives*

An F/A-18C flies with the F-35C, helping to develop tactical recommendations ahead of the aircraft's introduction into the fleet. Much of the early tactical recommendation were developed TOPGUN SFTIs, who were at the time assigned to VFA-101. The "Ghost Riders" disestablished and VFA-125 "Rough Raiders," at NAS Lemoore, is now the sole Navy F-35C FRS. *US Navy*

The Marines operated a single adversary squadron, VMFT-401 Sharpshooters, which flies F-5E/Fs. Located at MCAS Yuma, the Sharpshooters assist with the semiannual Weapons and Tactics Instructor (WTI) course conducted by Marine Aviation Weapons and Tactics Squadron One (MAWTS-1). They also help train new F/A-18 pilots assigned to VMFAT-101, the Marine Hornet FRS. *Fotodynamics*

This unusual paint scheme gives the appearance of much-narrower wings. *Twomey*

This flight line shot of six Skyhawks shows the different color schemes employed by VF-126. *Fotodynamics*

The Airborne Electronic Attack Weapons School (HAVOC) started in 2011 and drew heavily on the TOPGUN SFTI course outline in developing their own curriculum for Growler Tactics Instructors (GTIs). *Hunter*

Here an F/A-18C and F/A-18D fly a mission as part of the TOPGUN SFTI course. *Fotodynamics*

TOPGUN utilized the services of the F-14A/B Tomcat, F/A-18A-D Hornet, and the F-16A/B Falcon from 2002 through 2003. *Fotodynamics*

A nice overhead view of TOPGUN F-14A, F/A-18A, F-16N, and A-4M aircraft. *Twomey*

As was recognized by the 1968 Ault Report, the key to success is "the man in the box." TOPGUN has held true to this motto for over fifty years. *US Navy*